The Outdoor Art Room
Spring

Rita Storey

W
FRANKLIN WATTS
LONDON • SYDNEY

Franklin Watts
First published in Great Britain in 2015 by The Watts Publishing Group

Series editor: Sarah Peutrill
Art direction: Peter Scoulding
Series designed and created for Franklin Watts by Storeybooks
rita@storeybooks.co.uk
Designer: Rita Storey
Editor: Sarah Ridley
Photography: Tudor Photography, Banbury
Cover images: Tudor Photography, Banbury
Cover design: Cathryn Gilbert

Dewey number 745.5
HB ISBN 978 1 4451 3969 2
Library ebook ISBN 978 1 4451 3970 8

A CIP catalogue record for this book is available
from the British Library.

Printed in China

MIX
Paper from
responsible sources
FSC® C104740
FSC
www.fsc.org

Franklin Watts
An imprint of
Hachette Children's Group
Part of The Watts Publishing Group
Carmelite House
50 Victoria Embankment
London EC4Y 0DZ

An Hachette UK Company
www.hachette.co.uk

www.franklinwatts.co.uk

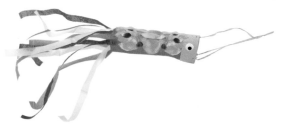

Before you start

Some of the projects in this book require scissors, sharp tools or
compost. When using these things we would recommend that
children are supervised by a responsible adult.

Contents

All about spring

Spring is a great time to get outside as the weather warms up after winter. This book is full of art projects and fun things to make and do outside in spring. Have fun!

When is spring?

Spring happens at different times of the year in different parts of the world. In the northern half of the world, spring lasts from March to May. In the southern half, it lasts from September to November. During spring the days grow longer. Day by day, the sun rises earlier and sets later.

In spring, the days begin to get warmer but the weather can still change a lot. Some days can be very cold and some can be quite warm. It is often very windy. Early spring days can see lots of rain showers.

What happens in spring?

Animals in spring

In winter there is less food about for wildlife so many mammals, birds and insects spend the winter asleep. This is called hibernation. Some birds fly to a warmer country for the winter. This is called migration. When spring comes and the days grow longer, the weather warms up. Animals in hibernation become active again. Birds that have migrated return home.

Many animals have their young in spring. The weather is better and there is enough food around to feed their young. There will also be plenty of food during the warm summer months for the young animals to feed on as they grow stronger before winter arrives. Grass that grows in spring is very good for animals to eat. Sheep have their lambs in spring to make the most of the good grass.

Flowers in spring

In spring colourful flowers bloom to attract insects. Insects go from flower to flower to feed on the flowers' nectar and pollinate the flowers (see page 24).

Bird nesting materials holder

Help the birds in your garden to make a cosy nest by giving them a supply of different types of nesting materials.

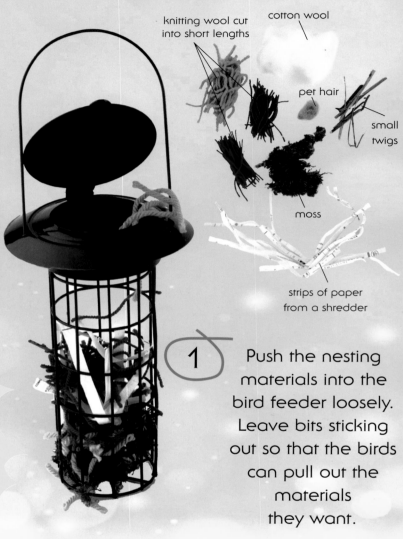

knitting wool cut into short lengths

cotton wool

pet hair

small twigs

moss

strips of paper from a shredder

You will need:

* a wire bird feeder
* string

a selection of:

* knitting wool cut into short lengths
* moss
* strips of paper from a shredder
* small twigs
* pet hair
* cotton wool

1 Push the nesting materials into the bird feeder loosely. Leave bits sticking out so that the birds can pull out the materials they want.

Birds' nests

Birds make nests to keep their eggs and chicks safe and warm. Different types of bird make their nests from different materials. The materials in your nesting station will make a soft lining for both eggs and chicks.

6

2 Tie a length of string onto the top of the bird feeder.

3 Use the string to hang up the bird feeder on a branch or window ledge.

Hang the feeder in a place where cats cannot attack birds while they are gathering nesting material.

The bird feeder can be filled with food once the nesting season is over.

Fish wind sock

Sometimes it is windy in spring. This fish wind sock will show you which direction the wind is blowing.

1 Stick the paper onto the card strip using sticky tape, as shown.

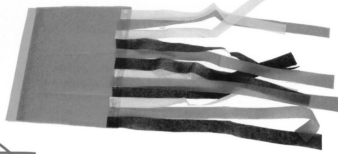

2 Tape the strips of tissue paper to the opposite edge of the paper.

3 Roll the paper into a tube and tape the edges together, as shown.

You will need:

* strip of thin yellow card, 6cm x 25cm
* piece of orange paper, 25cm x 18cm
* sticky tape
* scissors
* 1cm x 30cm strips of purple, orange and yellow tissue paper
* 2 googly eyes
* glue and spreader
* hole punch
* 3 pieces of raffia, 30cm long
* flower petals

Wind

Wind is moving air. As air warms up it rises and cold air moves in to take its place. We call this moving air 'wind'.

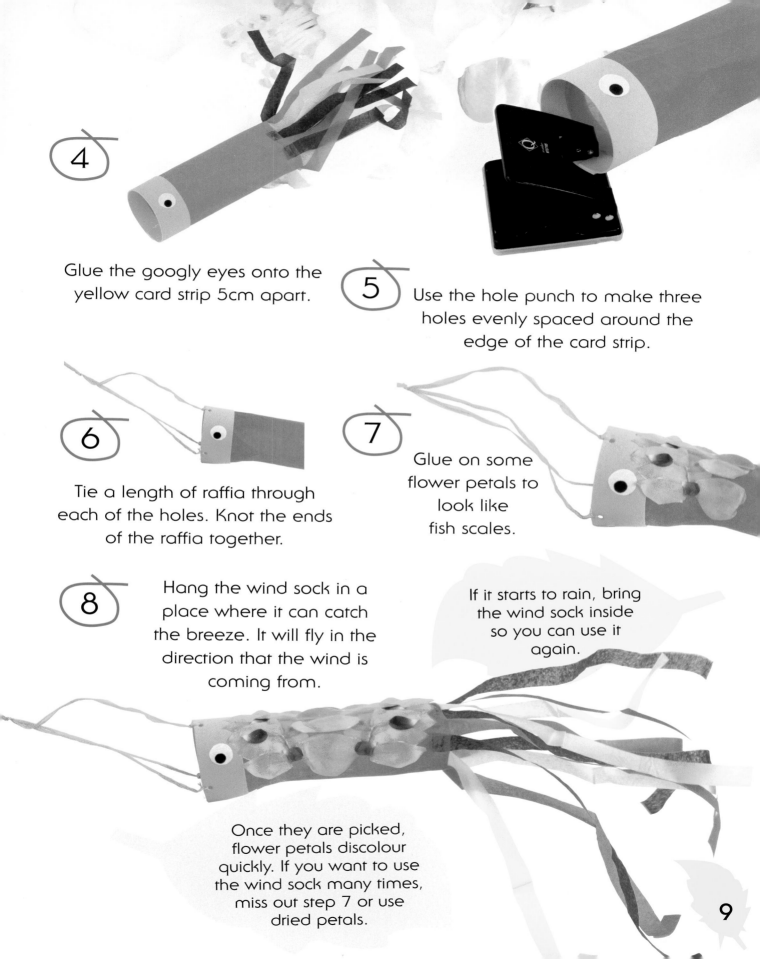

4

Glue the googly eyes onto the yellow card strip 5cm apart.

5

Use the hole punch to make three holes evenly spaced around the edge of the card strip.

6

Tie a length of raffia through each of the holes. Knot the ends of the raffia together.

7

Glue on some flower petals to look like fish scales.

8

Hang the wind sock in a place where it can catch the breeze. It will fly in the direction that the wind is coming from.

If it starts to rain, bring the wind sock inside so you can use it again.

Once they are picked, flower petals discolour quickly. If you want to use the wind sock many times, miss out step 7 or use dried petals.

Kite

This colourful kite is fun to fly in a light spring breeze. See how high it will go!

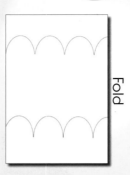

Fold

1 Fold the paper in half along the longest side. Use the pencil and thin white paper to trace the template on page 31. Cut along the pencil lines. Open out.

You will need:

* A4 sheet thin white paper and pencil (to trace the template)
* scissors
* A4 sheet of stiff orange paper
* A4 sheet of pink paper
* PVA glue and spreader
* stapler * hole punch
* 3 metres of yarn
* old felt-tip pen
* pencil and ruler

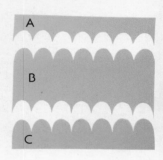

2 Trace around the template onto the orange paper. Cut along the lines, as shown, to create three parts – A, B and C.

A

B

C

3

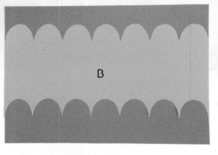

B

Glue part B onto the centre of the pink sheet of paper.

4

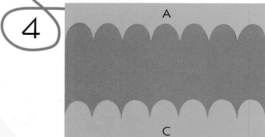

A

C

Turn the paper over. Glue parts A and C onto the top and bottom of the pink sheet of paper.

5

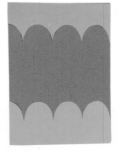

Fold the paper in half along the longest side.

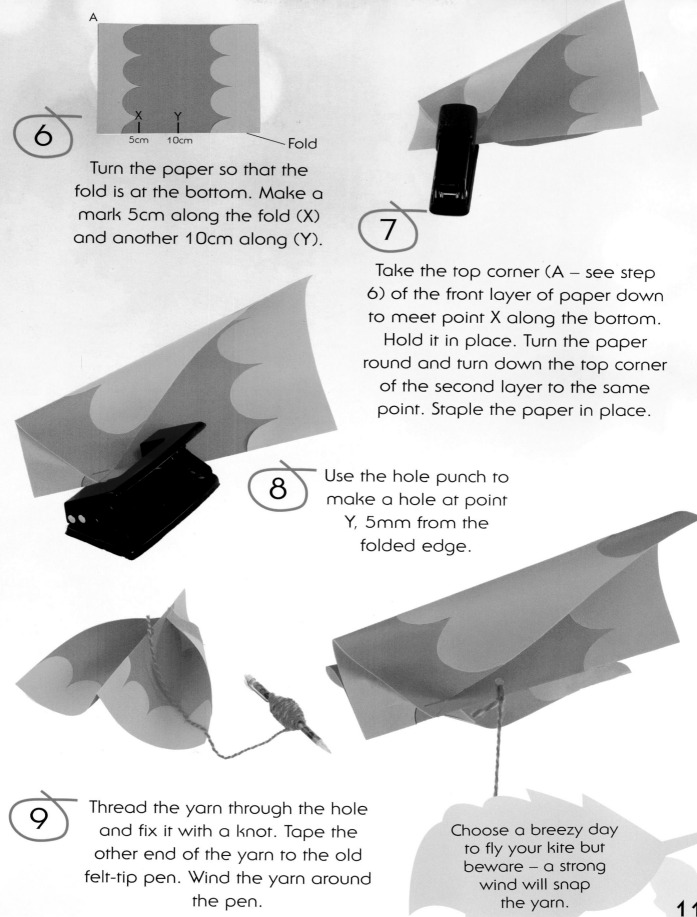

6 Turn the paper so that the fold is at the bottom. Make a mark 5cm along the fold (X) and another 10cm along (Y).

A

X   Y
5cm   10cm
                    — Fold

7 Take the top corner (A – see step 6) of the front layer of paper down to meet point X along the bottom. Hold it in place. Turn the paper round and turn down the top corner of the second layer to the same point. Staple the paper in place.

8 Use the hole punch to make a hole at point Y, 5mm from the folded edge.

9 Thread the yarn through the hole and fix it with a knot. Tape the other end of the yarn to the old felt-tip pen. Wind the yarn around the pen.

Choose a breezy day to fly your kite but beware – a strong wind will snap the yarn.

11

Grass hedgehog

This cute grass hedgehog will grow happily in your garden or on a windowsill. In the spring, grass starts to grow again because there is more warmth and light.

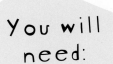

You will need:
* small plastic drinks bottle
* scissors
* an old sock
* trowel
* 200gm potting compost
* mixing bowl
* 4 tablespoons of grass seed
* 2 googly eyes
* glue and spreader

1 Ask an adult to help you cut the top off the plastic bottle. Recycle the remainder of the plastic bottle.

2 Cut 4cm off the toe of the sock. Push the bottle top through the hole, as shown.

3 Roll back the top of the sock. Using the trowel put enough compost into the sock to fill the top section of the plastic bottle.

In a bowl, mix the grass seed with the rest of the compost.

5 Carefully fill the sock with the seed and compost mixture. Tie a knot in the end of the sock and cut off any extra fabric. Water the sock section. Glue a googly eye on either side of the plastic bottle to make it look like a hedgehog.

6

Place your hedgehog on a windowsill or outside and water it every few days. In a couple of weeks the grass will grow through the sock and give your hedgehog lots of grass prickles.

Try mixing wildflower seeds with the grass seed to make a mini-meadow to attract insects.

Eco seed pots

These paper pots are ideal for growing plants from seed. When the seedlings are large enough you can plant them out into the garden inside the pot.

1 Fold a page from a comic in half lengthways. Use a ruler to make a mark on the cardboard tube 5cm from the top. Place the folded edge on the mark.

2 Roll the folded page around the tube.

You will need:

* page from a comic, magazine or puzzle book that you no longer need (the ones with non-shiny paper are best), 18cm x 25cm
* ruler and pencil
* cardboard tube from a kitchen roll
* seed tray
* potting compost
* flower or vegetable seeds

3 Fold one side of the paper roll across the end of the cardboard tube, as shown.

4 Repeat from the other side.

Seeds

A seed grows into a new plant. Seeds begin to grow when there is enough water, sunlight and warmth. Spring can be a perfect time to sow seeds.

14

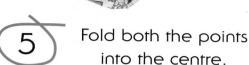

5 Fold both the points into the centre.

6 Turn the tube upright so that the paper pot is at the bottom. Remove the cardboard roll.

Repeat steps 1–6 to make more paper seed pots. Place the pots close together in a seed tray and fill each one with compost.

7

8 Sow a seed or two into each pot and water them. Place in a well lit area and remember to keep the compost damp. A few days or weeks later the seeds will sprout and grow into seedlings.

You can plant your seedlings outside inside their paper seed pots. The pots will break down and the roots of the plants will grow through the pots.

Mini greenhouse

Slugs and snails love to eat young seedlings. This mini greenhouse will keep a seedling safe until it is big enough to plant out into the garden.

1 Ask an adult to help you cut the plastic bottle in half. Trim the top part so that it fits just inside the bottom section and make a few small holes in the base.

You will need:

* 500ml plastic drinks bottle without a lid
* scissors
* red acrylic paint
* paintbrush
* yellow, blue and green acrylic paint
* trowel
* potting compost
* seedling

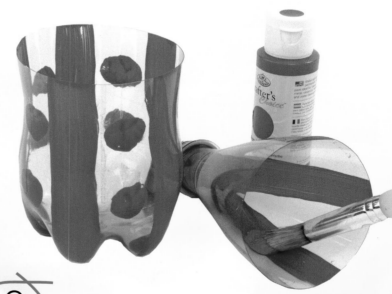

2 Paint a design of spots and stripes on the inside of the bottom part of the bottle. Paint stripes inside the top section. Leave them both to dry.

③ Finish off painting inside the bottom section using yellow, blue and green paint. Leave it to dry.

④ Fill the bottom section with compost.

⑤ Plant a seedling in the compost and water it. Put on the top section and place it outside. Don't forget to water it.

If the weather is very hot you can take the top section off during the day. Slugs and snails feed at night so remember to put it back then.

Plant labels

Use these pretty plant labels to remind you which seeds or seedlings you have planted, and what colour the flowers will be.

1 Ask an adult to cut across the paper cup about halfway down the cup. Put the top to one side.

2 Make cuts from the edge of the cup to the base, about 1.5cm apart. Fold out the paper strips, with the base of the cup facing up.

You will need:
* paper cup, approx. 10cm high
* scissors * ruler
* yellow and blue paint
* paintbrush
* black and blue felt-tip pens
* glue and spreader
* old felt-tip pen
* sticky tape
* red paint

3 Paint it yellow, leaving the base unpainted. This is the plant label.

4 Take the top section of the cup. Cut down the side from top to bottom.

5 Fold the section of the cup in half. Use the photo as a guide and draw half a butterfly on the folded edge. Carefully cut out the butterfly, cutting through both layers of paper.

6 Open out the paper butterfly and paint it blue. Leave it to dry. Use the blue felt-tip pen to draw a body and wing shapes.

7 Glue the butterfly to the label, as shown.

8

Tape the old felt-tip pen to the back of the label. Write the name of the flower on the white part of the label. Push the end of the pen into the soil beside your seed or plant. Repeat steps 1–3 and step 8 to make a second label. Paint this one red.

Weave a picture

Spring flowers can be very colourful. Pick some flowers in different colours and turn your garden or house into an art gallery with this colourful flower weaving picture.

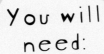

You will need:

* 2 sticks, 20cm x 20cm
* 2 sticks, 25cm x 25cm
* 4 short pieces of raffia (15cm x 15cm)
* 30cm length of raffia
* ball of natural wool yarn
* 3 long thin leaves
* some flowers with long stems

1. Place the sticks so that they make a rectangle. Use the longer sticks for the sides and the shorter sticks for the top and bottom. Tie the sticks together with short pieces of raffia.

2. Tie the end of the yarn onto the top corner of the stick frame. Wind it from side to side around the long side sticks, from the top to the bottom. Fasten off.

Thread a long thin leaf under and over the yarn from the bottom to the top (1).

Thread a second leaf next to the first one, over and under the yarn (2).

Repeat with a third leaf, threading it under and over the yarn from the bottom to the top (3).

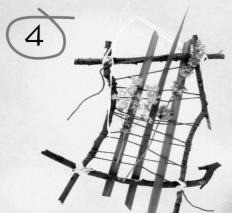

Tuck the flower stems in between the leaves and the yarn.

Tie each end of the long piece of raffia to the top two corners. Use it to hang up your finished weaving picture.

21

Windmill bird scarer

Birds love to eat seeds. To stop them eating the seeds that you plant put some of these sparkly windmills alongside them. The birds will be scared away by the moving windmills.

1 Fold the paper in half diagonally.

2 Then fold it in half again along the folded side.

3

Use the pencil to mark points 1cm from the centre along each fold line. Cut from the corners to the pencil marks (see dotted lines in the picture above for where to cut).

You will need:
* sheet of thin green paper, 15cm x 15cm
* scissors
* ruler and pencil
* blue and green glitter glue pens
* small bead
* sewing pin
* drinking straw
* adhesive tack

You can feed the birds with seeds in another part of the garden, well away from any seeds you have planted.

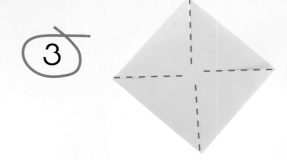

22

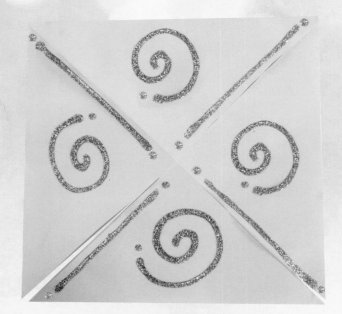

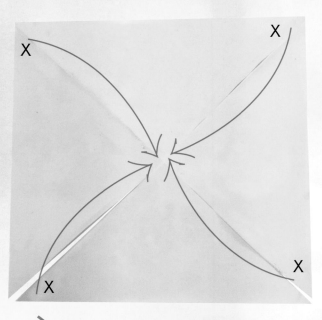

4 Decorate the paper with glitter glue. Leave to dry. Turn the paper over.

5 Fold the four points marked X into the centre.

X X X X

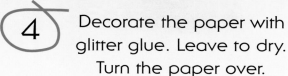

Adhesive tack

Pin

Straw

Bead

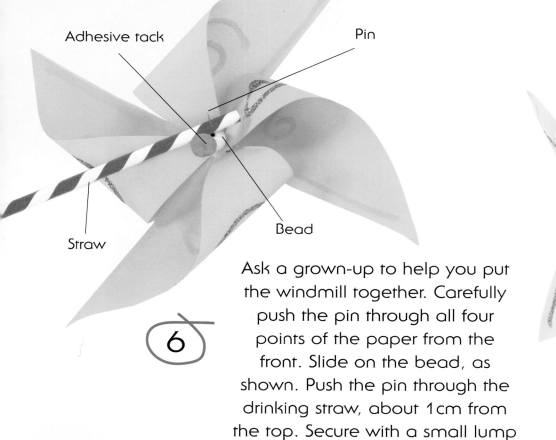

6 Ask a grown-up to help you put the windmill together. Carefully push the pin through all four points of the paper from the front. Slide on the bead, as shown. Push the pin through the drinking straw, about 1cm from the top. Secure with a small lump of adhesive tack.

23

Spring blossom picture

When the wind blows in spring, clouds of blossom fall from the trees. Collect some and turn them into a beautiful spring picture.

You will need:

* A3 sheet of blue paper
* thick brown felt-tip pen
* medium brown felt-tip pen
* fine brown felt-tip pen
* blossom
* paintbrush and PVA glue

1. Use the thick brown felt-tip pen to draw some thick branches.

2. Use the medium felt-tip pen to add some medium-sized twigs.

3. Use the fine felt-tip pen to draw some thin twigs.

Pollination

Blossom is another name for the flowers of some trees. Nectar at the centre of flowers attracts bees and other insects. As the insects gather nectar their bodies pick up pollen. When they visit the next flower, some of the pollen rubs off and a fruit begins to grow. This is called pollination.

4 Dab some glue onto each piece of blossom and press them in place to add blossom to the ends of the twigs in the picture.

5 Paint a 1cm strip of glue around the edge of the picture.

6 Press blossom onto the glue to make a frame around the picture.

Blossom pictures do not last for long so enjoy them while they are fresh!

Plant a dinosaur garden

This mini garden is full of herb and salad leaves. They are all good to eat so don't let your dinosaurs eat them all!

You will need:
* seed tray
* small stones
* trowel
* potting compost
* scissors
* cardboard
* kitchen foil
* small parsley plant
* lettuce seeds
* watering can
* cress seeds
* plastic dinosaurs

1 Put the stones in an even layer into the bottom of the tray.

2 Cover the stones with a 2cm layer of compost.

3 Cut out an oval shape from the cardboard and cover it with kitchen foil. Place it in the box. Cover the edges with compost to make it look like a pond.

4 Dig a hole in the compost in the top left corner. Gently plant the parsley plant in the hole, pressing the compost around the roots of the plant.

5 Sprinkle the lettuce seeds at the back and to the left of the foil pond.

6 Cover the seeds with a thin layer of compost.

7 Place your mini garden in a sunny spot. Remember to water it every few days.

8 When the lettuce seedlings are about 2cm tall, sow some cress seeds in the remaining space. Put your dinosaurs in the garden.

Parsley leaves, lettuce seedlings and cress are delicious in salads or sandwiches. Remember to wash them first.

Rain painting

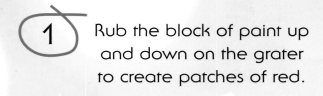

This is a great rainy day activity. Use the rain to make patterned paper. When it is dry, cut out some umbrella shapes. Tape the shapes onto the inside of a window.

You will need:

* 2 sheets of A4 white paper
* blocks of paint in red, blue and yellow
* old cheese grater
* thin white paper and a pencil (for tracing the template)
* scissors
* sticky tape

1 Rub the block of paint up and down on the grater to create patches of red.

2 Use the grater again to create patches of blue and yellow paint.

3 Keeping the paper flat, take it outside and put it on the ground in the rain. The raindrops will mix with the grated paint to make patterns.

28

4 After a minute or two, bring the painting inside and leave it to dry.

5 Use the thin white paper and the pencil to trace the template on page 31. Cut it out and draw around it on the painting to create umbrella shapes. Cut them out. Tape the umbrella shapes onto the inside of a window. Watch the raindrops run past the umbrellas.

Rain

Rain is water that falls from the sky. After it has rained, the sun comes out and warms up the land and the sea. Some of the water evaporates and rises into the air as water vapour. The water vapour forms clouds. Water droplets in the clouds join together. Eventually they become so heavy that they fall to Earth as raindrops.

Spring words

bloom when a plant comes into flower

blossom a flower or lots of flowers, especially on a fruit tree or bush

cloud a floating mass of water drops in the sky

compost rotted leaves, vegetable peelings and other natural materials

droplets small drops

evaporate to change from a liquid to a vapour

hibernation when animals go into a deep sleep to survive winter

insect a small animal that has six legs and usually two pairs of wings

mammal a warm-blooded animal that feeds its young with its own milk. Hedgehogs, bats and dormice are mammals which hibernate over the winter

migration when animals or birds move from one area to another every year, according to the seasons

nectar sweet liquid produced in a flower

petal the colourful part of a flower

pollen a fine powder found on flowers

pollination the way pollen is moved from one plant to another to allow fertilisation

seed the part of a plant that grows into a new plant

seedling a young plant

water vapour water that has changed from a liquid to a gas

weaving to make a fabric by threading strands or strips of something under and over another set of strands going in the opposite direction

Templates

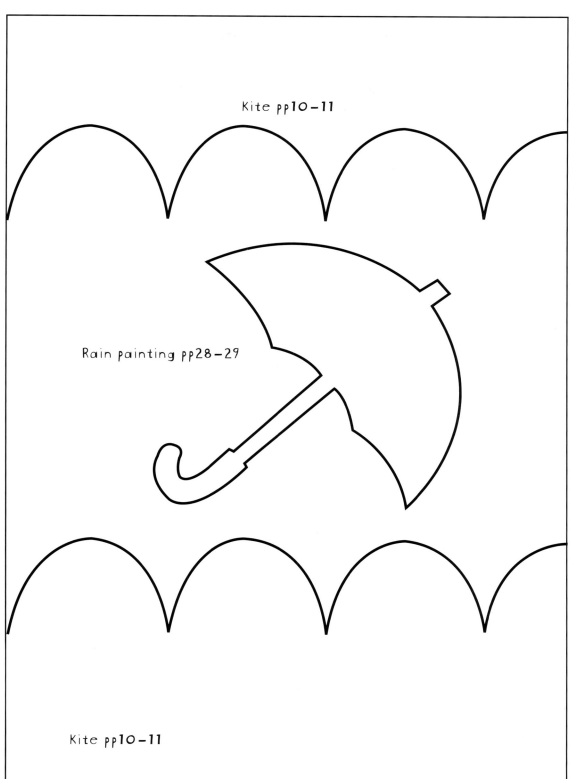

Kite pp10-11

Rain painting pp28-29

Kite pp10-11

Fold

Index

Find out more

www.dltk-holidays.com/spring/
Lots of great spring-themed crafts
and activities.

www.topmarks.co.uk/spring/
WhatIsSpring.aspx
Learn about all the things that
happen in spring.

www.naturedetectives.org.uk/
springwatch/
A set of activities put together by
The Woodland Trust
to get you outside in spring.

http://weather-facts.com/
seasons-facts.php
Find out more about the weather
and seasons.

Note to parents and teachers: every
effort has been made by the Publishers
to ensure that these websites are
suitable for children, that they are of
the highest educational value, and
that they contain no inappropriate
or offensive material. However,
because of the nature of the Internet,
it is impossible to guarantee that the
contents of these sites will not be
altered.
We strongly advise that Internet access
is supervised by a responsible adult.